WORK SONGS

poems by

Jonathan Cohen

Finishing Line Press
Georgetown, Kentucky

WORK SONGS

ACKNOWLEDGMENTS

Many thanks to these publications and their editors for publishing the
following poems:

Amethyst Magazine: "First Prayer"
Great Lakes Review: "Magic Feeling"
Naugatuck River Review: "Butcher Boy" (Third Prize, 2023 Narrative
    Poetry Contest)
Stone Poetry Quarterly: "Biology of Failure"

Many of these poems were formed in the gentle crucible of the PocketMFA
Program; thank you Josh Roark and Andrés Cerpas. Thank you, Clara
Cohen, Susan Lamb, Jim Nolan, and Kim Suneé for wisdom and
encouragement. Special thanks to Frank Paino, an inspiring poet, and to my
teacher Jon Davis: the moving finger writes and moves on, unless it belongs
to a poet, then it goes back and revises, again, and again, and again.

Publisher: Leah Huete de Maines
Editor: Christen Kincaid
Cover Art: "24 Hour Store," by Joe George
Author Photo: Chris Bartlett, Bartlett Studios
Cover Design: Elizabeth Maines McCleavy & Erica Heathcote

Order online: www.finishinglinepress.com
        also available on amazon.com

Author inquiries and mail orders:
Finishing Line Press
PO Box 1626
Georgetown, Kentucky 40324
USA

Contents

Experience is what you get while looking for something else.
Federico Fellini

Praise Song

Praise the first job
for what it taught you, the basic life-stuff,
more important, the lesson in decoding the essential self

Praise the *fun* those wearisome tasks created, the camaraderie
and friendships forged while stacking racks of hot dog buns
or risking the boss's ire by misplacing the new shipment of ice cream

Sing to the reliable drudgery and dreariness of sweeping
and mopping, exalt the freedom of mindless repetition prepping
the grill that respited school and homelife, and *everything*

Praise the bodily insult of early morning rising,
the youthful pride in learning to make change fast and accurate,
chant the first joyful feeling of *I am responsible*

Praise cleaning machinery on heatless cold spring mornings
when it seemed as if the sun had died seven billion years
ahead of schedule, plunging the world into total darkness

Lift voices to the new girl who joined the crew,
to juke box dancing until 2 at Circus by the Sea,
and, hey, Bill, let me drive the Camaro

Praise those tasks that shape the young and formless heart
Praise the first paycheck and pocket money, the first job
fired from, the first job quit, praise it all and be glad for the work

Zoo Concession Wise Guy

Furls of spun sugar wobble on paper cones.
Pink smoke hangs in the air, joins
the perfume of grill grease, soft serve ice cream
and sweat-stained, red-striped uniform shirts,
their circle-snap metal buttons failing.
From behind the opaque sliding screen, I thrust
the cotton candy at customers. Taking their change,
I mumble in my best Elvis, *Fuck you very much.*
Co-workers snicker. I tell them, make it sound
like *thank you* very much. Suzy, bold and saucy,
already has her driver's license—tries it out
on the next guy. Mr. Angry Dad yells at the manager,
What kind of operation you running here?
Suzy gets mop and bucket duty, throws eye
darts at oh-so-lucky me, assigned the gift shop
where I wrap a rubber boa around my neck, put suction
spiders on my glasses, juggle stuffed monkeys and laugh.

Elephant House Rapture

Across from the elephants
the kiosk red and
narrow as a London
phone booth luxurious

linden shade cream floret
carpet joins the tarmac
littoral like a flood

calm island in a sea of sticky
children bedraggled moms
a helium tank balloons
in brilliant circus colors

a wheel of dependable
twine the stolid register
room for a Coke
few customers, no boss

Butcher Boy

The day drops in another purple-gray sky,
headlights blink, tires spin in late winter mank.
The butchers, brothers, banter through the afternoon
about cars, dancers, money-making schemes.
Their assistant, a war-survivor given to fits,
enraged by late orders from old ladies, spits
in the chopped meat, smokes it off in the back room
with copies of *Leg Man*. I am good with pickling
tongue. I cut them thin on the slicer, steal a taste.
Otherwise, it's sweep and clean, sweep and clean,
take inventory, dress chickens, wrap a brick roast,
sometimes drive a special order, sit on the counter,
the counter, the counter, wakened but dulled
and dreaming. On break, I perch there, listen
to the brothers as they mutter about the imperium
of the oil cartel, the President's gimmicky call-in radio
show, exclaim the virtues of women they say they've known,
detail the cars they've owned and driven. One curses
the chicken man at the warehouse for bolloxing an order,
a daily rite. The other hymns a neighborhood legend
for his skill at cards, romance, business deals. They honor
their fathers by getting orders out to shut-ins after closing,
lighting candles alone in a storm, knowing there will be
no reward, that moving cases of black-market liquor,
tires, food stamps in bulk is the only way to keep
the lease, stay in the game. A brief squall peppers
the spreading dusk, adds to the slush clogging the avenue
that draws the city's ragged margin, sinking under the weight
of snow and the announcements of more job cuts.
Buffalo Forge. Republic Steel. Urban Milling. The dirty
snow liquifies in the heat of truck wheels, fissile material
in an unstable world, forms small mountains that explode
and reform, all gone soon enough. All gone.

Taxicab Blues
Variations 1-3

1.   *I Join the Company*

Mean effluvia, defeated vinyl seats,
denatured plastic molding, stale cigarette smoke,
encrusted spilled drinks. Sweat and menace thread
the air. At the garage one afternoon, Vic, a veteran
of Indochina, he likes to say, cracks to Joey,
the whippet hard dispatcher, about someone's
"old lady in the joint." Stay away from Vic, don't expect
a break from Joey. The whole fleet is like that—ex-cons
and petty criminals, T-shirts and jeans, heavy boots
even in summer, three a.m. pallor punctuated by tanned
driver's arm. I ask the drivers for advice: best place to idle
after an airport drop and no return, where to grab lunch
in the southern suburbs, all ranch houses and strip malls.
"You buy your lunch, kid?" Winter thin coyotes
with permanent hangovers and smoker's
cough vying for carcasses. I am a pup to be ignored
or jumped for a fare, which happens enough.
Get a radio call, pull up to the address, another
cab is there. Get on the radio, ask for a new ticket.
"Driver 9, what are you doing? I just gave you an address."
Long silence. "Driver 9, pickup from Hostess Restaurant,
Elmwood and North. See if you can close the sale."

II. *Meditation on a Regular*

Who can say how anybody gets to such a point,
making a daily ritual of dressing for lunch
at the Hostess Restaurant, three blocks west,
complete with hat, scarf, gloves, waiting alone
for a cab, to sit in a shadowed booth, tiffany lamp,

nibbling cinnamon toast, sipping tea hot and sweet
from a China cup and saucer, waiting for a return.
We know what this is, know it in our neolithic bones.
We understand without being told. The surfeit,
the extra of our limit. We stop arguing with ourselves,

stop wrestling with being, retreat to mind—it's not even
a question of fate. As sure as anything, as an animal
or an ancestor, compelled by the stars, the feel of the wind,
its scent. What choice is there but to pantomime
another life, maybe imaginary at that, of order

and cleanliness, purpose and respect, common
understanding. There is no need to speak much,
platitudes suffice when everyone plays their part—
"they do a nice job"—until the elevator breaks down
or the cab doesn't come.

III. *Cri de Coeur*

A pickup at university administration
gets in with attitude like most fares,
speaks in a low dismissive voice,
repeats the address loud and slow.
Fares don't want to talk, they have
places to go. I see this man's eyes
in my mirror—enraged, sorrowful,
he has been subjected to an insult
deeper than the sea. He is well dressed
in an academic way, clean sport coat,
rep tie smoothly knotted, a handsome
Black man going to fat and gray as if
he has been desk bound for the last five
years of his life, held in a leather binder,
draped in a London Fog overcoat, anchored
with good Alden wing tips. He rummages
through his papers, pats his coat pockets,
goes through his briefcase, rifling and prying,
opening compartments with ever greater
urgency, muttering now, cursing, hissing
hard consonants, spitting exclamation
points, violent wordless underscores.
Do you want me to turn around? I ask.
No, he says emphatically, his tone challenging
my very presence in his life, just let me out.

Jackie's California Diner at Main and High

Falling over my feet, I'll follow you all the way to High Street
—Mink DeVille

The hot corner where the world
comes to meet its wants and needs,
the bus stop a portal to another sphere
perhaps something new for Charon.
In the diner, Bill, the old cook, shows
me, three weeks on the job, how to fold
an omelet in a square. A malcontent,
he doesn't like tradition. Jim, mustachioed
manager, disco shirt, top button unbuttoned,
is counting receipts when a city cop orders
coffee to go from Barb, pretty and round.
He leans on the counter so he can look
straight in her eyes, says they found
blood on the wall of the Sleep Lodge
next door but no body. Everyone crosses here—
doctors, lawyers, hustlers. The TV bar
and the hoodlum bar, the biker bar all quiet,
only the bar favored by the printers' union
is open, because three shifts and they
don't go home. In my head, the *Drifters,*
Evie Sands. Easy, silent, I work the grill.

Assistant Cook Puts His Shoulder to the Wheel

I
The venison chef
killed and cooked held a bullet—
he took the week off.

II
The art festival crowd
like grasshoppers overwhelmed us—
we ran out of food.

III
I begged potatoes,
bags of wings from neighbor bars.
Got fired anyway

Disc Jockey Agonistes

I told you I had a show on the college station,
spun records for three nights at *Gabriel's*.

You said, most definitely, I can use you,
we need to bring the crowds back from the Boulevard.

You said I could play what I want, just keep it lively,
more rock than disco, but still some disco,

but mostly rock. That's what you said.
I said sure, this place is legendary.

You said just bring the crowds
tell your friends, jack it up, get it going.

Of course, no one came. Pizza and wings
happy hour specials attracted malingerers,

the clumps of guys who drifted along the avenue from
bar to bar, the gaggles of turned-out girls never showed,

the glamour or whatever had migrated. It was no
longer a cool place and never would be again.

I don't blame you for getting nervous, but
running into the booth every 20 minutes

shouting, play more rock, no, play more
disco, it didn't help.

Your punk brother and his pals sitting in
the corner making wise cracks, yodeling like Slim Whitman,

that was counterproductive. Time to go, we both
knew it, the one signal that didn't get crossed.

All the Summer Jobs in Chatham Were Taken

I left my favorite work shirt on a chair
in a friend's Northampton kitchen. I doubt anyone
noticed. Hitched a ride to Chatham where the summer
jobs were all taken by golden children
in polo shirts and woven belts. I quit that pleasant
beach town, stripped awnings talking to the breeze,

put it behind me for the sparse highway
in a gas shortage, headed for rain-soaked Maine,
sun to clouds, gray road, filling stations, diesel trucks.

Mother liked to quote Margaret Mead that
people are basically good, but I doubt she ever said that
and if she had, she had never been to Holden,

where a bunch of guys packed in a rusted Galaxie
tried to cut me down with tire chains as I stood
by the side of Route 1A like Buddha in a storm.

What else could I do but challenge my unresponsive
fate that way? Eventually an old man stopped—wet,
sodden duffel bag—we rode to Bar Harbor

and there you were, serving ripe, transcendent blueberry
muffins, leaning over fishermen's breakfasts
for tips and because you liked the attention.

I talked my way into a prep cook's job at the diner
on the square—plates of eggs for morning locals,
boiled lobster super cheap for frugal tourists.

A plastic eagle nailed to a tree on a harbor island—
you could see it from the kitchen. The owner, a short
French Canadian took me in more than gave me a job.

His son and nephew got on me sometimes, said
I thought I knew everything, was too proud to learn.
They were good guys and we had fun working together,

maybe Mom and Margaret Mead were on to something.
You shared your house and bed and friends with me.
We ate our own lobster from the dock next store and swam

naked in the waterfall's pool like natural gods.
Made our morning eggs with beer—cheaper than milk.
We saved no money, earned the wealth of kings in each
other.

Wonder Mouse

Let me tell you, the Times Square guys
are not selling umbrellas in a rainstorm
for the benefit of mankind. But Wonder
Mouse is another story, a source of delight
for all and a money-maker to boot.

On Park Avenue, in the block between
the Helmsley Walkway and Colgate Palmolive,
the Amazing Wonder Mouse will scamper
up the side of any building or dart in and out
of your coat sleeve. Every day, it's a well-heeled crowd.

There is no time for tricks or duds. Don't worry,
Wonder Mouse always delivers. The guy selling kebabs
from the Hallal cart on the corner? He has to drag
that gear back and forth from a garage in Flushing
while he lives in Bayonne. With Wonder Mouse,
that's not your headache. You could sell something else,

the climbing spiders, sure. They use a motor like what's
in the mouse. But nobody *wants* spiders; they're not cute.
A one-shot deal on Halloween at best. Newspaper stands?
Forget it. First, they are owned by conglomerates. You're
an indentured servant. Second, they're going out of business.
I feel for those newsstand guys, their world is dying. Hey,

I see your concern for the gray-haired woman retching
in the gutter, the sun blistering her milky skin—pay it
no mind—someone will come for her. You, my friend,
don't have to throw yourself to the fates so long as
you have Wonder Mouse. It sells itself.

Work and Play

I stand in a small park by the harbor
and listen to the winds

There are only two:
one is of the sea, the other the lake

One is death, the other play
regardless of the myths about four

In the saltwater wind I hear
the drudgery of oystermen, factory workers of the sea

The freshwater wind carries voices
of boys capturing frogs, building a bonfire

Work is death, paid out in morning
diesel fumes, lugged steel nets

wounded hands mixing blood with rain,
shells, the waste of birds and fish

Play is work, organize the game, cooperate,
skin knees, make alliances, quarrel.

Accomplishments are measured in things put together,
made functional. Fire is glory.

Often the winds howl,
signaling a violent depuration of the entire world,

tabulating life's stakes, the risk of becoming
a repeating whirl or misty evanescence

Big winds feel like history swaying on its hinge
Quiet winds toll our wins and losses.

Saratoga Road

This is the delight urban planners must
dream, the massive flow of cars,
trucks, RVs over unimpeded super courses
interconnecting highways stretching the Grand

Trunk Road, Kabul to Kolkata, Boston to Seattle,
across the region, the nation, everyone busily moving
like ants, of course, purposeful. Or small tributaries
and larger streams flowing into one great efflux

toward the sea, spreading commerce, alluvial riches,
subversive ideas, creative destruction. Like the four
by four pulling the sporty motorboat down from
the Adirondack lakes that didn't manage

the interchange, slipped now from its trailer,
ass-end in the verge. New transactions will unfold,
tow truck, mechanic, hotel, restaurant, souvenirs.
Dropping down from the north, following

cracking thunderheads, sailing above the spruce,
sugar maples, the yellow birch, signs for the Mohican
Motor Lodge, Fort Henry re-enactments, Lost Cause
Racetrack, the Tiki Lounge, Six Flags and the Dairy Bar.

Racing toward the hills of Troy, a light in the faltered
suburbs of innovation's diminishing campus. On the right,
the old, defeated capital, defiant in its ill-favored grime,
its odor of deal-making as old as the first Dutch trading post.

Pressing on to the Hudson Valley, the volume
reduced to county roads but still surging in all directions.
An air of rural ease, the pleasant nose of late summer
crops in the field, the farms and meadows not yet choked

but well ringed by shopping malls, hipster renovation,
gas-and-go marts. A quick stop at Stewart's across
from Hacket Farm Supply, coffee and a sweet
to fuel the last leg into Connecticut, Charles Ives'

tone clusters heralding a return to New England myth-
making, gazebo-centered town, spectral realities
enfolding, home to the briny coast. Travel done for now,
the trunk road awaits, orange cones, 2 a.m. flood lights, go.

Mount McGregor

I tried to bike there once, one thousand feet
of switchbacks to where U.S. Grant wrote his memoirs

to provide for his family, destitute, swaddled in blankets,
dying of cancer on the cottage porch.

At the park gates, an immense guard, a woman,
appeared in the middle of the road.

As I wheezed and gasped, she threw a meaty
hand in the air and said, "halt!"— like in a dream.

I never made it to the top, but when things were tough
from illness and ill fortune I took a job in the North Country,

moved my family up that way, worked hard and well
until the owner told me he couldn't make payroll.

There I was— dry-gulched and cheated,
my family stuck in a foreign place, angry, scared.

Mount McGregor loomed over everything we did
as we threaded that needle, saw it through.

We have moved away from the brooding pine forest
to the shore where sweet breezes blow in the morning,

bright roses bloom in the yards. No surprise, really,
Mount McGregor is here too, now like a following sea, driving us on.

Noir Christmas

There were no rooms near the mountain, so,
with the state capital emptied, my family and I took
an executive suite at the business hotel downtown. Most
restaurants and cafés were closed, the chocolatier and the tidy
gift shop where you could get something on the run for your
wife or mistress, buttoned up, everyone gone somewhere else.

We found a Nepalese restaurant for Christmas Eve dinner—
Vermont country décor and checkerboard tablecloths,
four of us nibbling on Thali and dumplings chased
with Green State Lager. A few knowledge workers
straggled in. Holiday orphans, they seemed okay with the hushed
sensation that we are not of the world, and it is not of us.

We headed home at a slow walk in gently falling snow,
our children running ahead, looking in shop windows, itemizing
goods to buy when things might open after the weekend. A group
of street people took over the town crèche, whooping and hollering
in their own Kingdom of Jerusalem, some arguing, some baying,
others blissed out or outright catatonic in seconded lawn chairs.

Back at the suite, gift packages were piled in the small conference
room—faux Eames sets, a large video screen. We gazed
on the town's festival lights showing dimly along main street,
the old-fashioned cinema's dark marquee communicating, it seemed,
telepathic messages to a bright moon rising over the parking lot,
revealing a woman from the crèche stomping out words in the new snow.

You think you know something, the words said, as she shouted toward the
street, at the empty offices, upward to the blue-black sky, *but you don't.*

Gypsy Children in a Fever Dream

As our director explained it, there had been
a corporate wobble, and the whole division was being
shuttered, 70 of us let go. I wandered the west side
of the city for days, zigzagging the blocks down
to Columbus Circle, milling among the kids

said to be larcenous gypsies, looking for something
to jolt me out of my zombie state. Maybe those kids were
pickpockets and thieves, but I saw no evidence. I will say
this: they seemed comfortable in their loose assembly,
congeries of fallen leaves skittering along Broadway.

Tired of following crowds, I called on the congenial
parlors of fortune tellers. Madam Sarah read my palm
in the usual way: *someone you love is distant and hard to reach.*
It was much the same with Madam Esmé. Madam Vadona
said she was from the Caucasus. I said I had been to Georgia.

She sneered, *there is nothing to do in Georgia.* The wine is good,
I said. *Yes*, she replied, *if you've never had wine.* Madam Kezia was
different. Job's daughter, the equal of her brothers, she spoke
with authority. She looked at my palm, said *your lifeline moves in
many directions at once. This suits you. Still, you must earn a living.*

Kezia directed me around the corner to *Fowad*, the store that
had no racks or shelves or bins, but hundreds of bargain shirts
arrayed in mounds on the linoleum floor. It seemed like a grand
experiment in chaos theory, deterministic patterns hidden
beneath mountains of cheap shirts. For a mere dollar,

a certain one would set a chain of events in motion, like
the butterfly that flaps its wings in the Taklamakan Desert
only to stir a hurricane on the Gulf Coast. I chose
a white button-down, wore it to an interview, got the job.
While I was returning from a meeting in Washington,

a hurricane washed out a trestle, stalled my train.
Endless hours piled up on the tracks until a group
of businessmen demanded to be let off—*our constitutional right*—
they insisted, but the conductor refused. Prying apart
the rubber bellows separating cars, seven of them

made a break for it, leaped onto the tracks briefcase first,
ran across a contaminated field, through a hole in a chain
link fence, and off into the mid-October afternoon. The world was
not expecting them as they slid toward the equinox, nor were they
prepared for what was coming. I waited with the others to be

bussed to a Baltimore hotel, a charming place on a quaint
cobblestone street in the Inner Harbor. There were coffee shops
and boutique stores, a florist, a boot maker, several fortune tellers.
I scanned the morning papers for news of what happened.
The businessmen had vanished. They didn't have gypsies.

Biology of Failure

Clenching shame is part of it, sure,
but so, unexpectedly, is bright freedom.
One draws the other, propelling toward
heightened awareness. That is to say,
self-awakened, alert. Beautifully exposed
to the world like an extending beach,
soft sand, pebbles, black and white,
sharp and smooth. Bright sun bleaching
washed-up kelp. Crabs, water striders,
in transitory tidal pools, this is their moment.
Purifying light warms and excites
before requiring breezes. Joy rides them
assuredly, vivifying redolent brine,
flecking sea-spray, miles of walking,
no voice or words, expanding hours.
Glistening riders bob the surf for waves,
daring fantastic triumph or spectacular fall.
A family wrestles happily with a kite.
Fragrant women align effortlessly
with the great curve of the earth.
A song everyone knows rides the air,
dies in the wind, revives,
fades before the evening star.

Magic Feeling

Oh, that magic feeling
Nowhere to go, nowhere to go
—The Beatles

It's been a career of failure since
I flunked math every high school year,
then drifted through summer make-up
focused only on certain important songs
like "Tighten Up," or "Everyone's Gone to the Movies,"
the floating bass line and scratching guitar,
the mocking smooth jazz, smart-alecky
xylophone jiffy-popping around deviant lyrics.

Time inures to terror, contemptuous looks, tense
family dinners that glance away like sleet
on a metal roof. What is gained: freedom
when the bottom drops away, the suspended edge.
Uncertain crossing, incomparable high, weightless
laughing. Not much more needed than
sturdy boots and a jacket.

And then digging out, the recovery. A new thing,
a project, a job. Growing stronger like the Hulk
smashing puny humans in the way,
amazing everyone with cat-like survival skills.
Exulting in sheer being, the world on its heels.
Reading a worn paperback about a Turkish harem
in a garage loft. Playing the flaneur on a late September
day, looking for Annette's house, clear, bright sky.

Then one day, I am sipping from a pint of milk,
lips luxuriating in the supra-white swill. Maundering
by the modernist music hall, fading statement
set against brick mansions from long ago,
sagging frame houses all around.

And I see, passing the music hall, an old man,
same size, build, same wire rim glasses, sipping
from the same pint of milk, walking at the same pace,
going the opposite way.

Before Leaving, a Memory

I found my mother's childhood
home online—the narrow frame
the crooked steps, the Tuscan columns

There were photographs
of all the rooms
we entered together one by one

She showed me
the stairway landing
where she mooned her parents' guests

the window
she climbed through to gain
a tree and hide a whiskey bottle

Best, I suppose, to forget
the gaudy Christmas mornings
but not the mechanical bird

or the air gun my grandfather gave me
loaded with soft mud from the front
yard, it made a great sound against the porch

memory is cruel that way

First Prayer
September 2019/ Elul 5780

These are the last nights of open windows and cricket sounds.
Mornings, the ground is soaked with dew.

We traced the path of Jupiter and trailing Saturn all summer long,
and now we can't find them, hidden behind jumbled night skies.
We work out winter's warning to buy a new shovel,
and salt for the driveway, to get some overshoes, wondering,

will Orion be a bright sign or a fading signal when
it crowns the southern sky?
will it signify our blessed fortune or a final notice of decree
from the Bureau of Fate?
the one that says, this is to inform you that you are screwed.
Let us make our appeal.

Imitation birdsong is the most ancient prayer, they say, the source
of human speech. Tamil Brahmins have chanted it for ten
thousand years.

I have mantras, too, as old as the oldest ancientness.
I stand in the yard listening.
I watch the breeze climb the treetops.
I prepare to pull the boat down to the shore.

To the deep we go, to petition, atone, face the facts,
to meet what will come with cheer, if warranted,
with resolve if required.
To tip my keel on the rolling sea—

the last open window, the last cricket song,
the first prayer of the soul's new year.

Jonathan Cohen is from Norwalk, Connecticut and Buffalo, New York, where he held many of the menial service jobs-short order cook, butcher's helper, taxi driver, concession stand worker-that inspire *Work Songs*. His recent poems have appeared in *SALT, Image, Cloudbank, Stone Canoe Journal, I-70 Review*, and others. He is a winner of the *Naugatuck River Review* Narrative Poetry Prize, a finalist for the Ralph Angel Poetry Prize, and a finalist for the Richard-Gabriel Rummonds Poetry Prize, as well as a nominee for Best Spiritual Poetry and the Pushcart Prize.